Que Sera, Sera

by

Harmony Hagadorn

Angelo,
Thank you for
your service, I hope
you find one thing in
here you enjoy.

DORRANCE
PUBLISHING CO
EST. 1920
PITTSBURGH, PENNSYLVANIA 15238

Dorrance Publishing Co
585 Alpha Drive
Pittsburgh, PA 15238
Visit our website at www.dorrancebookstore.com

ISBN: 978-1-6393-7049-8
eISBN: 978-1-6393-7838-8

Que Sera, Sera

To those men and women who shared the load with me:
Existence feels lighter with you.

BLEEDING

If I could, sometimes
I think I would pry my ribcage open,
Pour scarlet to these tainted pages,
And inhale the sting of
A solid breath.
I am suffocating.
If I could, sometimes
I think I would gouge the eyes
Resting tired in my skull
And drain it hollow
To wait for tears to evaporate
That I have yet to shed.
Let me tear this canvas down and pull these scraps through bleach:
Clean my slate; let
This body be a sterile wonderland
By sunset,
Or so melt into the earth below
By sunrise.
I am tired;
Let these bones rest,
Hanging loosely.
Of my body, the scarecrow
To ward off the demons
That make it through all defenses;
Finally, be the peace and take to the soil.
Sleep, little one.

CREDITS

At the end of the movie, the audience sits aghast.
Several hours of this masterpiece,
A conclusive scene,
And a black screen—
Lurking eyes meet
The other curious patrons.
Where were the end credits?
How are we to know
How this came to be?
The years of work that was crafting this thing
That came to be
Behind the scenes.
I guess what I am trying to say
Is, how awkward it is
When everyone can share this amazing film
And have no one to thank?
Let your life be this movie:
Every breath anticipating a next moment to this media.
No one just "came to be";
We are not accidents to happen upon.
Give credit to your story,
Everything that is a part of you.
Give yourself some recognition.

STEPS

You're standing,
Looking out and down to the high tides over the higher cliffs.
You are no longer scared;
The steps to the edge are
Scarier than the cliff's end.
As you look down, notice the swell of the ocean,
Mother's heartbeat;
Let her arms lift, pleading to take you home.
Your heart, a mighty conch
Fear no more—
There is only relief once the feet rise from the ground.
Crash with the steady shore,
Evaporate on the way down,
Becoming dew on the blades of grass/
Return home;
Inhale, and simply relinquish all pain
In your body.
It is not your burden to carry.

PILLOW TALK

In this restless slumber,
I often twist and turn,
An unparalleled hell.
Pins and needles
Prick at my fingertips;
Pluck vibrations into chords of my bones.
Play a symphony,
Hoping to hum me
Back to sleep.
These nightmares
Are starting to sound
Like lullabies.
How am I to know
What is real anymore?
Paralyzed frame
Pumping steam,
Bleeding exhaustion;
So many melatonin memories.

V.

When you asked me how I knew I loved you,
What I said was your humor.
Oh, how I missed the ache of laughter,
The warm caress of a stir in my diaphragm.
I know that to be only a partial truth.
How did I know I loved you?
The safety in occupying this breath with you,
The steady slowing of my heart rate as we laid entangled in moonlight,
My body rising to shake hands with peace.
She is a new acquaintance
I now know by name;
These jitters are lulled
Steady by honey-soaked
Words, dripping sweet soliloquies, filling conversation.
Love, take all the space.
How could I not love you?
The patience paid directly to me,
Signed on the dotted line;
Cross your T's and dot your
I-I-I love you's.
Give yourself some credit:
In this lifetime,
There are many things I may never understand,
Copious contortions of controlled manipulations
And sputters of deceit
Floating discreetly by in the wind;
I may never know how the creation of man came to be.
My only understanding that
From a mother, came you, and I
Can settle in this ignorance as long as it doesn't nullify
Your presence in here and now.
I cannot count these stars to know how many constellations;
Illuminate this blue marble we call home.
But I do know that doesn't matter.

When you asked me how I knew I loved you, and I laughed,
Simply, I wasn't sure at that moment I had
Ever known anything else
On this blue marble.
Lassoed by the gods' sun-kissed freckles called stars,
You are what I call home.

SWEET YOU

I remember thinking,
She must be from a big family...
How remarkable it was,
Her love for competition,
And I was a challenge.
She was captain of debate team:
Let's fight about all of these things;
Those words are never breath wasted.
I remember fighting about the seasons.
"The winter," I said, "was so bitter and brittle,
A blanket of suffocation,
Frigid and numbing, a
Cold temptress
When the sun slept early, and I
Yearned for release."
Telling her of my hollow heart,
She stayed smiling.
"But what about
The designated time from the divine for fireside conversations?
And warm cocoa,
Hugging pillows of sweet?
What about cute mittens
And snowball fights?
The glitter from the clouds sprinkling our lashes,
Decorating us, so they dazzle, waiting in anticipation,
Perched under this seasonal mistletoe."
God, how I love the winter
And hate the spring.
"Allergies," I said,
"Leave me in a state of disarray;
The bugs!" I squealed,
"Take liberty to take my personal space as their own."
Before my next breath,
Her soft tone

Wrinkled my complaints
With a folded paper airplane
Crashing down into this void signed with
The words, "Flowers would disagree," so side with the flowers, I did.
In the next instance I felt my face grow red; flaming.
Anger mimics this heat wave.
"How unfortunate we are to exist in summer?
Sweltering,
I see sidewalks boil;
I know our concrete jungle craves sweet release from the sun.
This sticky moment
Bleeds beads of sweat;
Think how I miss relief."
Hands over her ears,
Laughing, she said,
"Think of sweet ice cream cone memories
And late-night firework shows,
Lighting the fire for
Summer love;
Tanned skin during sand.
It is a nice day at the beach;
It is basking lakeside,
Rope swings to infinity;
The nostalgia of 'summer break.'"
"The fall then,
When all living things shrivel to dust.
Let our trees shed;
Mother Earth is dying."
"Change!" she boasts,
"Is necessary for all of us.
Perhaps
Let this mean a clean slate,
Wipe us pure and
Prepare to rise again.
This is simply the universal time to better yourself."
By the end of our fight,
Like many before,

I was motionless,
Mesmerized, a glass half empty.
I had been begging for someone to fill me up when she
Simply grabbed the glass and held it to the light,
Proclaiming in its magnified glow:
"An overflowing cup
Would simply be harder to balance."
Spinning the crystal,
My darling says,
"You see half empty and wish solely for satiety;
I see crafted art, still in one piece.
Still serving its intended purpose.
Still does not drain.
This art is half full and as sturdy as the day it was blown.
Perhaps it's not that you are missing anything
Aside from the perspective to see more than this volume itself.
There are many things in our tainted worlds to love;
We learn from the part of the story we focus on."
My optimist.

DEAR BODY

It is me. It is you.
In this moment we spend,
I am aware of the crescendo that is
The rising with the inhale
And the fall of the exhale;
Let these frail ribs hug
My lungs,
Keep me safe so that
When I finally remember how to,
I can breathe.
When I draw the curtains
Of my eyelids, I sit
Only with the song of my heart,
Steady drum.
Thank you for the symphonies in my fingertips;
Fingertips, how you hold these words!
I love the masterpieces you muster;
Create something from nothing,
A true genesis.
Simply write
Thank you to my ears
For hearing all the "I love you's,"
And even all the "I hate you's"
That mold this body into the statue she is.
Stand tall but never still;
These feet that carry me
Feel the sand on their underbellies,
Run through grass with innocence.
Thank you, nose, for the warmth in the smell of grandmother's baking,
Making memories.
Thank you, body,
For bridging this mind,
Keeping my head above every wave crashing down.

WITH THE SUNRISE COMES SUNSET

I awoke this morning to find I never did;
Death reached his cautious hands down to me,
Outstretched to bring me home,
While I laid in silence contemplating.
Looking back,
These bones turned to the world beneath me,
And I watched those ants dance.
For hours, he waited for me,
A short price for my new lifetime
In a distant universe.
Stopped in a nursery to remind myself
Of new life, laughter
To will good fortune on these cradled juveniles;
May they never know pain or sadness.
Floated my spirit through the great barrier reef,
Sat at the bottom to feel the tides pull over my being;
So powerful, so full of mystery, this dark mistress kept hidden.
Death turned to me slowly, and in a slow deep voice, this echoed:
"You knew the inevitable this whole time
Never ignorant to my presence, you were given time
So why, small human, did you waste it?
Why did you turn away the kindness
You always deserved?"
Taken aback, I dropped my head to respond.
"Living on the inside often felt like living on the outside.
I spent too much time waiting and wishing for the sun to rise
That I never appreciated the stars."
I awoke this morning to find I never did;
Death reached his cautious hands down to me,
Outstretched to bring me home.
If I could do it over,
I would enjoy the simple things over;
I would accept those I don't like and embrace those I love,
Dance barefoot in the woods,

And sit still for a moment to give myself grace.
I was so tightly wound; I would learn to let go.
We are all born damned to die, but we control what we do in the moments between.
Not every second has to count;
But we can't afford to be cavalier with our souls.
Live in good company, child, should you wake again.

REFLECTIONS

I look down to a little girl
Tugging at my sleeve,
Eyes tired and screaming for help.
This moment we share is silent.
"Little girl,
Where is your family?
Why are you alone?"
Looking around now, I see
This chaos unfolding around in this surrounding world,
I must've blacked out,
I must've pulled the alarm.
I don't remember, but I can hear the cadences of bells
Pinging to the lights in this least-inspiring orchestra of panic.
I must've blacked out,
I must've pulled the alarm.
I don't remember, but I am running.
I look down to the little girl,
Tears welling in the emeralds;
I knew I smelled smoke.
We are locked arms, standing in our burning circus,
Searching for an exit,
Searching to save this little girl.
Reflections dance in this hall of mirrors;
The noise levels rise, and I can feel my heart in my throat,
Beating to the steady sirens.
"Little girl, we need to save you.
Where is your family?
Why are you alone?"
Eyes dart back towards the funhouse mirrors
I must've blacked out,
I must've pulled the alarm.
I squeeze the hand of this little girl to tell her she is safe.
I smell the smoke
My fingertips slip loose and drop to oblivion,

And I now see in these many reflections
In this frantic house of horrors.
It is filling with smoke; through these clouds, I see
There is no little girl,
Only this woman who
Must've blacked out, must've pulled the alarm.

NINE-ONE-ONE

This echoing alarm sends
Shivers through my spine,
As if my body was anticipating
Chaos all along.
Before I am aware,
These hands are outstretched,
Sliding to answer
Through the daze of this 2 AM hour.
I listen to
Sputters of threats and concern.
It is another human I have
The pleasure of calling friend in this lifetime,
Hiccup crying through the telephone wires.
Despite any early mornings
Ahead, I rise with the occasion and make tea
To settle into this conversation,
Heart dripping with sweet
Words melting
Like chocolate,
Telling them of their worth.
While my stomach churns
As the cocoons hatch,
Filling my lungs with butterflies,
I calm the feeling of
Beehive hands by sharing a silly antidote,
Empathizing with the wound,
Or simply taking space.
Tell them to think of
These great galaxies,
Scattering stars
Shining light onto
Little blue matter.
It's all matter.
It all matters

To hold a mirror to
This wounded deer
And direct its gaze to all the wonderful things in and out,
All the blessings
Residing in this body called
Home.
Laughter is such an understated gift;
So much so, we forgot,
Or better yet,
Feel guilty for the many things that
Make life worth living.
Reminder to you, that you
Are allowed to be happy,
Are allowed to feel pleasure,
Are allowed to laugh
If your mind allows it.
We are not designed to run on this hollow ache alone.
Do not be fooled.
Why are we only ever special in our miseries?
The six stages of grief flicked throughout our time together,
Hypnotizing hypothesis of
"What if's?"
"Should" is a swear word.
I can tell by the
Tone in their voice
That reality is surrounding
Them once more
Out of this impulse,
Wave set for destruction,
Crawling back towards
"Maybe one day, it'll all be worth it,"
And that
Hope hangs like a lifeline.
Hang up
And stare at the flickering 03:17
On the bedside table;
Pray to whoever

That they may find
Some rest tonight.
Because I know these thoughts
Continue to race,
Front row seats for
A trip down memory lane;
Including the calls that I missed
And the somber black-tie parties preceding.
Can't get them back,
I lay envious of those who possess the strength
To pick up the phone in the first place.
Blessed I was chosen
To be on the receiving end,
And horrified that
When the time is up,
I won't have the same
Bravery set in stone
In these fingertips to dial.
Snuggled in these ashes,
Burn down the safety net,
Hoping I was a disguised phoenix all along.
Come to find, I missed the course on rising.
How programmed this broken record plays,
Ready to save those
Of us with the greatest pains.
Oh, ballerina, tip toe,
Pirouette this dance of
Hypocrisy;
Feel the stage light
Searing the face.
Mimic the sun
With the breeze through
The wings.
I hear echoes in this
Empty auditorium
As I approach first
On center stage,

Ready to illustrate just
How easy it can be
To just be
Happy,
Content,
Loved,
Aware,
Safe.
It is not so heavy with the help of a lent ear of shoulder
To bare these tears,
I promise.
Watch me
Glide off from the spotlight with the illusion that I am
Nearly
Floating,
And you can, too.
Blissfully unaware of how much strength
Goes into
Keeping this frame from
Collapsing.
Then, spotted from above, this ballerina never made her call,
Left floating from
The rafters,
Released to fly once more;
Her phoenix moment.
This was never the intended rise.
Don't let it be the rise and fall,
The illusion of a feather like a ton of bricks.
Gravity was never our friend.

WE SIT

Car packed full of people,
Eyes telling me our souls
Have never been strangers.
Windows down,
The breeze kisses
Our faces like a first love.
Returning home,
Music loud to
Drown the thoughts
And all smiling
Despite the deep
Secret of our mistress.
Depression
Keep her calls at bay
For this moment alone;
Speed past these
Remarkable people,
Filling other space
With thought and stories.
This complex
Car ride
With no destination;
Though by daybreak,
We may all be broken.
In this instance,
We are
Beautifully intertwined
In this memory alone
And the warmth
Filling our usually frigid spirits.

LOOP

To have lived a thousand lifetimes
Is to have died
Nine-hundred, ninety-nine deaths,
Nine-hundred, ninety-nine black tie events,
Masquerading this,
Mourning for
Tears never wept at my expense.
It is with every death,
A moment of reflection
Paralleling my bent,
Over-bargaining
Promises of one more chance.
It is with every death,
Learning new ways of laughter and love
And finding other damned souls
To share this burden with,
For by nightfall,
Do not weep in
Sour nostalgic tears.
Rather,
Look to this as an
Investment for
Many you's that have yet to inspire.
Don't let the expiration
Of who you were
Be the weight
Laid to your ball and chain,
Sinking you into the sea of "should."
You could not have
Done anything differently;
Wishing to is
Often a waste of such few breaths granted.
Destiny, whether you call her by
Myth or truth,

Is the one left standing
At the funeral,
Ready to lay the flowers,
Repurposed,
For the next breath you draw,
Anticipating
The first day of
The rest of your life.
Don't let the odds be that
If I have in fact lived my thousand lifetimes
And died my
Nine-hundred, ninety-nine deaths
That they all be in vain.
These figures
We inhabit
House these fragile souls;
Let not this be an illusion.
Death is certain, but
The only way it maintains its validity
Is simply
By having to have lived in the first place.

BREATHING

When the curtains fall forward,
I am able to drift to
Neverland,
Shut off the lights,
Lower the volume, and
Inhale the sweet
Moment in peace,
So consumed in thought
That no thoughts
Arise,
Telling your tired eyes
To open, and you can rest.
It is 70 degrees, and the breeze is playing
Tag with the sun along the
Curves of your face.
This moment
Is safe.

PLEASE LET ME GO

"I'm not crazy," she said,
White knuckles rest pressing
The outer thigh.
Eyes fill with red wells, and
Skin begins to exhaust.
"I'm not crazy," she said,
Room bubble wrapped,
Tied with a bow signed:
"Don't even think of questioning us."
After all,
They knew her better.
"I'm not crazy," she said.
We almost believed you
that time; try again.
Later, when your socks
Aren't non-slip, this
Hell where we
Keep your laces,
How could you not
Feel safe in this
Building where
Everyone is trained to belittle you?
After all, I would.
Think this feels like home?
"I'm not crazy," she said.
Laughing fills the hallways;
Other prisoners—I mean, patients—sit,
Eyes glazed over.
How many tranquilizers
Can we gift like
Candy before
A code blue?
Just enough to keep them breathing.
No one is really here.

"I'm not crazy," she said
Sure, I'd believe you,
But that's exactly what someone who
Is crazy would say.

TRICKS

"Shall I turn on some music?"
His pursing lips curl
Upwards to a smile
As he gently lifts
The needle to the record machine and
Depresses it on the rim
Of the spinning disk.
Reaching for the volume,
He nimbly twists it clockwise,
Filling the room with noise.
"Hello," it says.
"This is my name," it says.
"I am okay," it says,
And on repeat plays the story of me.
Keep on,
Keep on,
Playing and
Re-re-repeating
This tale of a broken girl.
Flip the record,
Scratch the disk;
It sounds the same in any pitch.
Each time forced
To hear my life play on
Loop until I
Am so sick and tired of
My own story that
I beg for it to stop.
I think it is time to change the narrative.

PINOCCHIO

Tiny little puppet
Tied to my tiny little strings,
Let my mind control you;
You'll do anything.
Tiny little puppet,
Dance in a masquerade,
Fooling all the people;
Happy's a charade
Painted bright, white smile.
Monkey say, monkey do,
I choose all your actions;
Make these thoughts come true.
Tiny little puppet,
Why do I see you weep?
Wipe away those tears now
Before they think us weak.
Tiny little puppet,
See this world made just for you
Underneath for me,
But soon you'll see,
There's nothing you can do.

EASE IN PAIN

Shame is not best enjoyed in solitude;
Rather,
It can be the shared experience to spark
Human connection.
The burden is no longer carried alone;
Our vulnerabilities will save us.

AN ODE FROM AN ABUSIVE MOTHER TO HER DAMNED DAUGHTER

I promise I heard crying,
Dearest daughter of mine;
I ran in here to find you,
To prove that I am trying.
Up to the crib, quick paced and out of breath,
I reached my arms to grab you,
But there was nothing left.
I promise, I remember;
I promise, you are real.
Invisible dearest daughter,
I kiss and sign this seal.
I have been busier and busier
As each day does pass us by,
So consumed in all the living,
Hyper-focused on these lies.
I promise, I will find you,
Just slipped out of my grip;
These trembling hands stay shaking;
This stomach sinks a pit.
Dear little girl, can't find you,
Grown up and grown too old.
Dear girl who never calls now
Learned to build her own home.
The panic in my heart now
Beats faster at its best;
The ache of missing you now
Chokes me half to death.
I wish I'd paid attention
To the crying all along.
Please don't think I abandoned you,
Though I know it's wrong.
I should have said, "I love you";
I should have been aware.

The time has gone unnoticed
Because I wasn't there.

CLOUDS

I float for hours,
Suspended six feet over this shell of a body,
Watching for any sign of life
That never comes.
It is sitting at a table with friends
Who don't blink an eye despite
The lack of my presence so heavy, I might as well not be there at all.
I watch this body
Clean and feed itself and continue to survive as if surviving off muscle
memory alone.
It is the same thing;
The same thing;
The same thing;
The same thing
As always—
I am screaming at this borrowed cadaver,
Tearing at the very seams that hold this puppet together.
I am screaming to get up,
To go outside,
To move,
To do anything but lay here and be trapped inside my own mind.
I am just here,
A void space shuffling around this busy world
Bumping into;
Bumping into;
Bumping into
Strangers in passing,
Two parts of empty,
Looking for something to fill them,
Looking for life.

OLD BONES

My life, chaotic as it is,
Is all I have known,
So don't be surprised when I find
Beauty in tornados or broken mirrors;
They feel like home.

GREY AREA

I am a grey area,
Both bold and anxious,
Full of rage and passion;
I am so angry and accepting,
So calm and chaotic,
Everything as is and in between.

US PAST MIDNIGHT

This isn't how it was supposed to play out;
I haven't felt this way ever, and there's no rhyme or reason that now
It has to be you;
But it does.
But,
How can I forget something that never even happened?
How can I erase all the things you didn't say but I needed you to?
How can I move without the feel of the touch that I can't even
remember?
But I remember it all,
And I've never even felt like this before, so I just feel stupid now,
Because I know you don't even think of me anymore.
I know I was never enough for you
And that your life kept moving, and you don't dream of me anymore.
But how can I breathe knowing I am nothing to you,
And you were supposed to be everything to me?

MAKESHIFT MAPLE SYRUP MEMORIES

I had a dream last night that my parents were still married,
That this November, they would be celebrating 20 years of true love,
That I grew up believing in fairytales because I was living one,
And I rested my head easy every night in the same bed for 18 years.
I dreamt that suitcases were for vacationing to the grandparents,
Not a home for me to thrive off,
That I would fall in love one too many times my senior year of high school
And be sure that, this time,
I couldn't recover from this heartbreak—
And I did.
Through a summer love up at the lake, somewhere with good friends
And a little too much stolen whiskey that smelled like grandpa's breath.
But not Dad's.

In my dream, my parents were a picture of perfect.
They would have quarrels now and again, however, nothing that an
apology couldn't fix;
And it did.
In fact, in my dream, apologies were granted when deserved;
They weren't a compromise of pride.
They were a part of a healthy vocabulary,
One where I grew up understanding that sometimes I was wrong, and I
had to admit defeat;
And sometimes others were, and I earned their sorrows. I deserved their
apology.
They were not rare; however, they didn't consume me because—

In my dream, I never lived a life of regret:
I kissed that boy that I liked
When I snuck out of the house and had one too many wine coolers;
I crawled in through the doggy door and found my sisters,
Now on their second year of college, discovering themselves through
whatever drug of choice.
In my dream, my brother has a girlfriend who is kind and supportive.

My family loves her so much, she was in last year's Christmas card.
But not everything is peaches.
In my dream, I fail a test,
Lose a best friend,
Crash a car,
Get fired,
Break a bone,
And just find myself existing like everyone else.

I had a dream last night that my parents were still married.
Their love tasted like coffee grounds and Sunday morning pancakes
And burned like cigarettes,
But I made it out alive and went to college, as it was supposed to play out.
In my dream, it was never a question if they loved me or how I was gonna do it,
And in real life, I guess it isn't either.
Quite simple really:

They didn't,
And I did it because I had no choice

BERMUDA

I want to disappear,
Find myself on a road map leading to 25.0000° N, 71.0000° W,
The center of the Bermuda Triangle,
Submerged under the water with other wrecks, so I won't feel so alone
anymore.
I want to sail to Atlantis,
Ten-thousand feet under, where light can no longer find me
And the sun is just a myth,
where silence is the loudest noise for miles.
My ears will not ring;
My head will not burst from pressure,
Because my whole life I've already become accustomed to suffocating.
I want to vanish,
Walk alongside Amelia Earhart,
Talk with Perry Saturn,
Relate to Casey Kasem.
I want to vanquish from mere existence,
Be buried six-feet under if it means I can get away,
Spend my life in a bunker, unaware of how the world is functioning
without me there to watch it
Crumble,
To never see doomsday because mine came so many years before.
I want it to travel to the center of the Earth,
Scratch at the clay and feel ridges of fossils poking my spine;
To evaporate into thin air
Like the thousands of tears I've shed;
To wane with the patterns of the moon
And melt away to a memory

CREAKING

I open up,
Not like a book no one has yet to read.
My spine is worn from people trying,
But I am no book with words set in stone in an order that's not quite how
it happened.
Chapters aren't how I would describe my existence.
This pain knows no end or last page number to tick your finger across,
discovering it's over.
It's not over.
I opened up more like the steel hinges coming undone on a cage that left
its parasite die inside,
Forgotten;
I tried again and again to forget
I am the one who let the door close behind me,
Putting myself in the cages for you to bat around.
Hey, Babe Ruth, I'm tired of the sound of the metal rattling,
But it's all I've known.
I let you hurt me, and I suppose that's on me.
It's my fault that I continue to open up;
It's my fault that I find my mind to be naïve despite broken-record style,
Repeating all your wrongs.
I put in ear buds of symphonies between "We are okay" and "We will be"
To drown out the sounds of your wrongs, and the bat keeps hitting my
cage,
And I fall shamelessly again,
Like I never see it coming.
Insanity is doing the same thing over and over, thinking you'll get
different results.
So, admit me then;
I keep letting you in over, and over and thinking you won't break my
heart.
I am losing my mind, trying to figure out yours,
And just whenever I think you're opening up,
The cage closes behind me,

And I'm left insane, ticking tally marks on sides of concrete slabs as my sentence.
I used to think the world of you, Mom,
But this world isn't one I want to live in anymore, and you're to thank.
I'm opening up,
And every time, you rip at pages, leaving marks I can't correct.
You pull chunks from my story to twist into your own.
I'm sorry for the next person who wants trust;
I don't deserve it.

AN ANOREXIC LOVE

My bones are hurting because I haven't eaten in 48 hours.
I sleep most of my days away because I have no energy
And am just about disappear altogether.
"But I am not hungry," I say;
I turn down every meal
I drink water to fill my stomach
And count calories in my toothpaste.
I have never been like this...
Why now? Why me? I don't know, but I am dying, and I can't ask for
help.
But I'm screaming, "Save me!"
I've said no a thousand times and sleep through lunch at work every day,
And yet no one catches on.
"I just have no appetite,"
Slips off my lips,
But I watch them devour food,
And I am jealous and angry.
I am weak.

CLEANSING

It's not spring, but I've been cleaning all day:
I've cleared out all the photos of us,
Deleted the messages,
Scrubbed clean my calls,
My voicemails;
Erased video after video of us laughing,
Not understanding how it happened.
And I'm clean now.
But it still hurts.

WHOLESOME

I myself am not a person;
I carry a piece of everyone I have met in my veins, those I have loved and
hated.
I am every late-night car ride
And sweet ice cream cone memories.
I am stitched together by the apologies I did and didn't receive,
Every accidental argument I overheard from two parents who couldn't
find love anymore.
I am every server I have tipped,
Every hand I've held,
Every constellation in the night sky.
And while I still feel every hand I have told no,
It is secret handshakes between friends;
It is my first kiss.
My person is every interaction
Compiled into the carcass of too much emotion.
All of my friends,
My family,
My enemies,
And strangers;
It's no wonder it is fragile!
It will take time,
But this body is written beautifully and has taken years to change.
I love every person who is a part of it,
And perhaps that's all I need to love it as well.

TWINS

Love and pain are brothers birthed from fear
That subsides in our guts, clawing their way out;
Both so bad and so necessary,
So natural,
They stem from our roots like wild flowers in an overgrown garden,
Sucking nutrients from the soil they reside in;
So powerful to cause nuclear war, and it has,
And it will.
Love and pain are identical,
A two-way mirror that leaves love blind to the fact that the only thing
between it
And it's brother
Is a thin sheet of glass.
They are anchors wrapped to our ankles, dragging us to a pit of unknown,
Through an ocean of tears already been cried for people who don't
remember how we taste when
Our names roll of their tongues,
Down into reefs filled with regrets,
To a point where monsters roll from their sides,
And destroy all the fish in the sea we never saw coming.
Love and pain are transparent;
You see them in everyone,
Banging hands crawling up your esophagus eager to get the next words
out, but
You bite your tongue, and your eyes scream out like sirens speaking
volumes.
The problem is that
We are born with pain running through our blood, ready to spill out at
the scrape of a knee
Or a heartbreak,
But love is learned.
Love is nurtured for much longer and overrides the
Amplified feelings the petrified poison of pain brings.
It is stronger,

But it also results in it;
Turns the tables, turns your heart into its brother's hands
If you left it with the wrong person to begin with.
They pour from a person's soul,
Love and pain, and the brothers birthed from fear.
They leave us vulnerable,
And that's what makes it beautiful.

SWATCHES

This is a poem for the colors in life no one stops to appreciate:
For the monochrome slate that lies beneath my feet and borders buildings,
That creates empires,
And smooth as it stands,
Ever so stern,
There is beauty in its simplicity;
For the green of the moss taking root in sides of wide oaks
Or in streaks barreling down hills,
Purifying the water for us to
Indulge;
It's the yellow of the taxi
That adds color into a jungle of asphalt and concrete
That is so familiar and yet so foreign...
It means you're going somewhere,
You're moving forward, moving on;
And the white covering walls,
Fresh paint in a new house
Made to look clean and pure,
And while it will not last,
Is just white
And subtle nothingness.
This is for the understated colors,
For so many more
That define the universes we build,
The pigments of life.

A REMINDER

I sit at the bottom of the pool,
My body curled up into paper balls of notes being passed through an
otherwise silent classroom.
My lungs lay deflated towards the bottom of my rib cage, caressing my
diaphragm,
Eyes shut to reveal only darkness,
Ears ringing from the pressure of the water weighing in on me.
At peace with the water
And despite my fear of drowning, I remain stationary until my eyes bleed
red, and
I can no longer contain myself, and my lungs crave for the taste of sweet
oxygen again.
I must be so close to drowning
To make myself realize that my body
Still wants to live,
That I still want to be here,
And I surface once more for a gulp of relief.

SACRIFICING

You are a mess;
And trust me, I know a one when I see one.
I myself am spilled tomato soup on a clean kitchen,
An egg shell bit that broke off into the otherwise perfect omelet,
Sour milk you forgot to throw out when you went out of town.
I'm a leaky trash bag that reeks of beer spilling out of God knows which
way soaking your feet;
I am shattered glass on carpet,
Clutter in a hoarder's house building up,
A soda machine broken left pouring out on to the floor,
And God knows I pour.
I define mess,
Make tornados look like amateurs;
A natural disaster so
Natural, I paint my face a mask.
But you are a different kind of mess:
You are a gum-ball truck that spilled over on a highway so hard to catch
And yet you can't help but to stop and smile.
You are a kitten unraveling a ball of yarn;
You are walking so blindly into love and coming out of it so changed.
You are a mess,
But I will always be waiting with paper towels and brooms
To pick up the pieces left on the ground.
I keep steel wool on me to scrub what I have, too,
So you can see for once that you aren't a mess like me.
You will raise hell;
You will spill over;
And I come back every time, willing to destroy the pieces of myself I just
glued back on
With gloves on, ready to get my hands dirty
And damn, I would let me shatter if only to be able to pick up your pieces,
To pour what's left of my chipped glass and old milk
Into yours so you aren't empty.
But you are a mess.

1111

I guess you could say I'm
Craving for someone to be head over heels for me,
To learn the curves of my body despite being as consistent as the waves.
I want someone to feel deeper than undiscovered oceans when they hear
my name
And find themselves gasping for air when they see me,
Jaw dropped,
Eyes full,
And just consumed in me.
Teach me to love me like you do;
Discover new worlds that have been impeding from my fingertips
unknowingly.
Train me to be more patient
And dream of my smile.
I need someone to appreciate me like the princes and princesses in every
story book
And, when the sun goes down,
Someone to hold me;
To listen to my words and build castles from them;
To pick up the ashes left from my aching body, which I have burned,
And just lay with me in silence,
As if every breath I took next to them was the ending of a grand
symphony.
Not to shower me with gifts,
But knowledge,
And challenge me;
Someone to love not only my body, but my soul.
So yes, I'm craving for someone to love me;
Someone who makes the planets swing full circles in a masquerade
As the days float by as if no time has passed
And miss the taste of my lips when they release, if not but for a brief
moment to gasp for air.
We will spend so much time consumed in one another
That our very ears will forget the sound of anyone else we've ever heard,

And we will flock like every love song is written for us because we feel like our love is
So unique yet so bold that we deserve movies: Our happily ever after.

SHE STILL HAS NOT READ THIS

I'm sorry, Mom,
I got so caught up in life that I forgot to stop along the way to say thank you;
Thank you for your undying love,
The indescribable glow and warmth your smile emits.
Thank you for holding my shaking bones when they withered late at night
Because I was never as strong as I thought I was;
For being my first line of defense,
For being compassionate and patient,
For being my mother.
I'm sorry, Mom,
That I let people's words get to me,
And that I heard their voices drown out your screams;
That I heard their flaming insults and believed every word that they spoke
From the daggers that hang from their mouth, spitting poison.
I'm sorry, Mom,
That I spent so many years
Not believing you
When you told me that those people were bad for me,
Because I was so consumed by fitting in and feeling like I belonged that I
pushed away the one person who loved me unconditionally.
And I'm so sorry, Mom,
That I found comfort in places you told me never to look
And that I found myself down the same path that you once took despite
you warning me
Over and over and over and over that it can't it can't, it won't
Do anything for me.
I'm sorry I stayed crying in my room
For weeks at a time,
That I spent countless hours with my face buried in my pillow as to muffle
the sounds
Of my tears hitting them like glass shattering,
That I laid defeated for years so alone,
An island

Among so many others,
And that I never once thought to come to you despite your hand
Reaching down towards me to pick me up as if to say,
"It doesn't have to be okay, but you don't have to be alone."
And I'm sorry that at some point, I was embarrassed to hold your hand because I have
Half your DNA flowing through me in an ever-growing family tree
And sprouting at my fingertips, and yet I couldn't let people think that I,
A teenage girl,
Could be anything but rebellious and malicious towards her own mother.
But I love you, Mom,
With every fragment of my being,
And I will crumble when you do.
Thank you for being my crutch for so many years and giving all of you
Until you were nothing but a small freckle of dust floating in space.
I'm sorry, Mom,
But you are my sunshine.

THE MYSTERY OF HOW I MADE IT THIS FAR

When I was young, I wished so badly to just be 16 already,
To have a boy love me like I thought my parents loved each other.
I wanted longer lunch and less recess because I thought if I stopped
playing,
I would grow up faster,
But when time passed and life threw curveballs at me,
I wished it had stopped so many years ago,
Like a scene in a snow globe.
I realized that everyone you say "I love you" to won't say it back,
That you won't pass every test, even if you study,
That you won't be someone special just because you have always rooted
for the underdog,
Only to find yourself in the same situation.
I thought that everyone died of old age, so peaceful,
And in the night they just slipped away.
It wasn't until I attended four funerals in one year that I realized that
death is inevitable.
I thought that every time I threw the ball across the yard, my dad would
catch it;
Now, I find only my empty hands scratching at the back of the house
That I thought was mine until I saw them invade
I thought the neighbors were neighbors until my brother was sharing a
room with one of them,
And my father was sharing a bed with the other.
I thought that Santa would always eat the cookies we left, and get
everything on our lists,
But much like other things in my childhood, that idea died long ago,
When the tooth fairy stopped coming,
When the boogie man was no longer a threat.
I miss the innocence of a child, the same one I lost so long ago when I was
so focused on
Wanting to grow up that I never took the time to balance pros or cons,
Rights or wrongs.
I just wanted to be 16,

And upon being so...
I just wanted to be gone.
Words to remember:
I don't stifle myself for others' convenience.

DARK

When the darkness closes in,
When you become absorbed in the silence,
When you have nowhere to begin again,
That's when you let it in.

THE FIRST EULOGY I EVER WROTE
MARK

This one is for the solider
Who taught me to be a little bit braver,
Who showed me how to shoot a target and hit it,
Who gave me direction and took nothing but devoted obedience for an answer.
This is for the man who has seen hell
And returned with a smile and only memories and laughs to share.
This one's for the father
Who loved his kids to where it hurt,
Who took us on adventures to places we have never been,
Who showed us how to fix a bike or how to drive.
This one is to the husband of my mother,
Who has given her endless adventures, four bonus children, and four grand-babies;
For the one who woke up every day devoted to helping and serving her,
And doing whatever possible to make sure she was never lonely;
Who saw a woman in grey and brought color to her life and heart through the hundreds of roses
Over the years and filled every vase possible;
Who spent every moment of silence reminding her of her grace and beauty,
And how she was loved
He draped the room in jewels and perfumes of so many smells.
This one is for the savior
Who helped in times of trouble
And gave advice;
Who provided for us when something needed to be done,
Who fixed the broken toilets, no matter how nasty,
Who stayed and helped my mom every week when we left and brought her endless smiles.
This is for the man with endless love to give,
Touching souls from every continent,

Changing lives and saving lives.
He was selfless to the core,
Even risking malaria.
He would give everything to see someone he loved feel whole.
This is to the love story I got to see grow;
I saw the fights and the flowers to follow,
And I saw the Starbucks every Sunday and movies on Tuesday.
I saw the support and the tenderness and the concern he showed to every situation;
I saw the stories from across the world.
This is for Mark,
The butthole since the day he arrived,
For the man who yelled sometimes and used funky words we have never heard,
Who I called to flaunt his extraordinary accent every chance I got,
Who would wake me every morning as 5:00 by bumping into my door.
For the deaf man he is,
For making jokes from every situation and bringing light to everyone's lives,
The man who had given my mom slight abandonment issues
And set the bar for any boy or man trying to love any of us.
A genuinely passionate person, with the largest heart I've ever seen.
For someone who gave me a whole new family, who will remain my family.
This is for the man who, if he couldn't be good, was very, very bad.

FAMILY PORTRAIT

Raised on the failed expectation of a marriage,
Left with only fragments that left me frugal, and dependent on the
thought
That something better can and will come to those who work,
And the idea driven into our hearts that we are nothing more than the
ring on the table that was
Worn down with every drink my father had,
And the fact his problems derived from us and could only be secluded by
that of a beer bottle,
And the story from the lips of a delusional child who spoke
Of two people madly in love, only to shortly discover that her reality was
more than
"I love you" could bandage.
And the day they shared their separation, she didn't even bother to cry
from embarrassment that
All her stories of "true love" or "I miss you's" were all figments of her
imagination,
Along with the lies fed to her when that boy she once yearned to spend
every waking moment
With was gone due to one mistake—
One of which was less of a mistake and more of a habit that she had
learned
From the only things that were considered to be guardians.

VIC DAMONE AIN'T SHIT

The first time I smoked a cigar I was 18;
I thought it tasted like coffee,
And you made fun of me.
In fact,
You liked to make fun of most things that I did
Or thought,
But at the end of the day, you always cared.
You were the first person to believe in me for a long time;
The person who would build me up and break me down all in the same
breath.
A tough shell of a man
With the kindest soul.
You were the first person to ponder the stars for hours with me and still
have the audacity
To say that nothing is anything.
Everything is as is, and I should stop looking for metaphors in the clouds.
You were the first person to teach me that there is good in this world,
And there will be people who will use me
And who will hurt me,
That there are good days,
But some people have good intentions for no reason,
And that I had been over-analyzing people until I believed they couldn't.
But you kept insisting;
You never asked about my past
And said that I mostly wore my pain around me.
That I spoke,
And wrote,
And drew
Everything you would need to know.
I turned my brain inside out and painted it on the walls;
You said I could rule the world
If I could learn to use my gifts and knowledge;
It wouldn't matter that I was young.
You reminded me that the past is not a cripple nor the future a crutch,

And I could take the Lazarus of my body and rebuild from whatever I had
been
And open book with few words.
You saw it all:
The good, the bad, and the ugly,
And still believed in me,
That you would read whatever book,
Or listen to whatever song,
Or study whatever art
I had created.
No matter the medium, you would be the first in line to experience it.
While in any other world we don't meet
Or get along,
Because the chances were one in a million,
I am glad that I met you in this lifetime,
And though our time was short,
It was what we needed.
On your last night, you swore you would never forget me,
And I don't think I could forget you.
Thank you for every lesson.
May your journey be everything you wanted from it.
The last time I smoked a cigar I was 18.

THE ITCH

I have to have control,
So sometimes that means I have to be in charge.
Sometimes, it means I have control over what I do or don't eat.
*If I do or don't eat.

ARIZONA SKIES IN AUGUST

My clouds will swell with rain and pour onto these pages,
Washing away stories at a time.
Let me be the monsoon to bring life to a barren desert;
I promise you will hear my thunder

GET UP

There will be "just" days;
There will be days when you feel that existing is asking too much of you,
That if breathing was optional, you could not even muster up the energy
to do it.
You would sit in the silent state of suffocation.
You would stop your heart for beating, if just for a day or two.
There will be days that getting dressed might as well be travelling to the
sun,
That moving will disrupt the very clay beneath us
What I have learned from these days is that every victory is still a victory.
If the most incredible thing you did today was wake up,
Then let's celebrate your head leaving the pillow like its New Year's,
And this is the count down to the ball drop that is the rest of your life.
You can let your wilted figure rest but know that there is more to this
world
Than the moment you are living in. You will bloom.
If all you manage to do was stumble to get water, then let your feet
Hit the ground and take off running as if you're crossing the finish line,
First place at the Olympics.
Let every movement be a part of this choreographed ballet you called
today.
If you have to stretch that small feat all day, then let it be.
There are victories in every second you remain here.
Sometimes participation trophies are the only ones we need.

360

So far past okay that I venture to say yes.

18

Being young, sometimes I am naïve,
But believing I am less because of it only makes you ignorant.
Do not dismiss me simply because you have seen more sunsets than me.

NO

Depression isn't a trend;
It's forgetting what it feels like to go to bed without salty lips,
Still wet from the tears that lull you to sleep.
It's not just "sleeping in";
It's not being able to conjure up the strength to lift your head off your
pillow
Because of the gravity of this ever-sinking world.
Anxiety is not cured by just
"Not thinking about it";
It festers like a sore;
It is walking past a group of friends laughing
And knowing they are laughing at you,
Because nothing in the world could possibly be funnier than you at that
moment.
It's puking for hours, fearful of seeing your family;
It's scratching at your skin till you bleed because you just can't hit the itch,
Which is buried to far under the skin that it wouldn't help anyway.
It's inside your skull;
Bleeds red in your eyes when your tears dry;
Rips at your stomach like a starving lion.
It tangos with your brain until you are too dizzy to remember
Why you're shaking anymore in the first place.
It's a fault in the brain,
Something just off enough in our minds,
Displaced a little too far to the left
Able
To destroy an entire existence.
It's a medical condition that pills only make worse;
There is no cure for this pain.
It is habilitated in rehabs,
Where they take all the knives and rope from us;
They sit us in padded rooms,
In the quiet,

Not knowing that that is the one place that does the most damage.
When you are alone with only your thoughts, it
Brings more pain than any blades writing in cursive around your arms
could ever urge.

WHEN YOU SAY MY NAME, MY ENTIRE BODY RECOILS

I cringe.
Your tongue is a ship, and my name is the venom dripping from the end,
ever so sweet;
I hate that you made me hate me.

DAD

What hurt the most is when I would drive past your house
So slowly,
I could see into the window
And at that moment feel so shattered.
I realized that time had not stopped for you like it did for me,
And your world kept spinning with them,
And I am not a part of it.

PINK MIST

My life blew up too many times to count,
So I stopped trying to fix the pieces,
I stopped trying to find the pieces.
I stopped.

US

I don't wish you well;
I won't send sincerest regards;
I won't call.
I'm over wasting breath on telling you we can still be friends.
I'm over nice—
I want to watch you fucking burn.
I want you to know the pain that I felt;
I want you I know that you hurt me.
I don't wish you well;
I wish you out of all of my memories,
Out of all of my stories I let you into,
Ruining moments of my life that were once so happy.
You took so much from me,
Drained my body of every ounce of energy,
Kept demanding more,
And I let you every time.
Don't call or text;
Don't accidentally send messages to me,
Or drive by my house.
Get out,
And stay out.

IT WAS ALWAYS A TEST

I crossed my fingers,
Knocked on wood.
I carved the answers into every conversation,
And you
Failed me every time.

REBOOT

I killed myself to be the person you always wanted,
Cut chunks of my personality and buried them with every flaw.
I did everything you asked of me and more:
I rebuilt myself time and time again,
Hoping that the next version of me would suit you better.
Nothing was ever good enough, and I finally remember thinking,
This time I am creating the version of me that I want,
One where your name has been erased from my memory, and I am me as I
have ever been.

FAMILIAR...

I can remember the lines in the palms of your hand,
I know the sound that your footsteps make,
I can smell your freshly washed hair,
I could tell which detergent you used,
And I keep retracing the shape of you in my head
When I held your heart in my hand and let it slip through my diligent fingers,
Taking so much time to study you and remember you.
This is so strange now, because I want nothing more than to forget
You, and my mind just won't let me.